SRA Reading Mastery®

Transformations

Reading
Textbook A

Siegfried Engelmann

Owen Engelmann

Karen Davis

McGraw
Hill

Acknowledgments

The authors are grateful to the following people for their assistance in the preparations of Reading Mastery Transformations Grade K Reading.

Joanna Jachowicz
Blake Engelmann
Charlene Tolles-Engelmann
Cally Dwyer
Melissa Morrow
Toni Reeves

Emily Jachowicz for her valuable student input.

We'd also like to acknowledge, from McGraw Hill, the valuable contributions by:

Mary Eisele
Nancy Stigers
Jason Yanok

PHOTO CREDITS

8 Fuse/Getty Images **11** (t)McGraw Hill/Ken Cavanagh Photographer (b)McGraw Hill **14** iStockphoto/Getty Images **35** Ingram Publishing/SuperStock

mheducation.com/prek-12

Send all inquiries to:
McGraw-Hill Education
8787 Orion Place
Columbus, OH 43240

ISBN: 978-0-07-905360-2
MHID: 0-07-905360-2

Printed in the United States of America.

3 4 5 6 7 8 9 10 WEB 26 25 24 23 22 21

i e a i o i

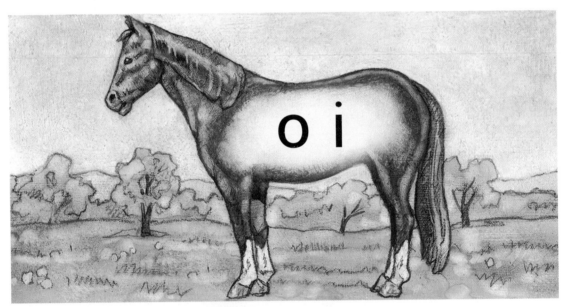

o i

 <u>no</u>

<u>me</u>

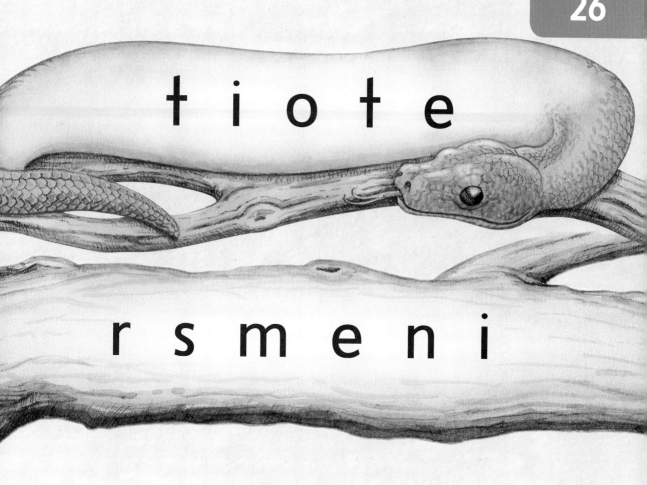

t i o t e

r s m e n i

<u>so</u>

<u>no</u>

<u>see</u>

 a e t o t i

 e r l n o

1. <u>see</u>

2. <u>me</u>

3. <u>no</u>

lafsmor

1. <u>me</u>

2. <u>see</u>

3. <u>seem</u>

etoita

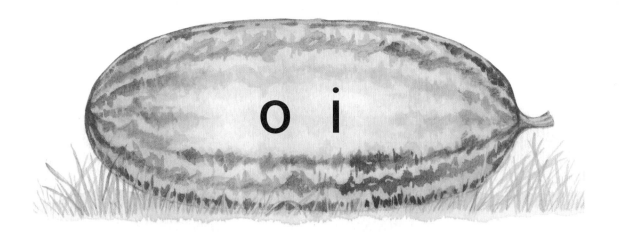

o i

t p i p o

e r f n l s a

1. <u>seem</u>

2. <u>so</u>

3. <u>feel</u>

e i o

p o a p

<u>ll</u> <u>nn</u> <u>ee</u>

<u>or</u>
<u>for</u>

<u>me</u>
<u>see</u>

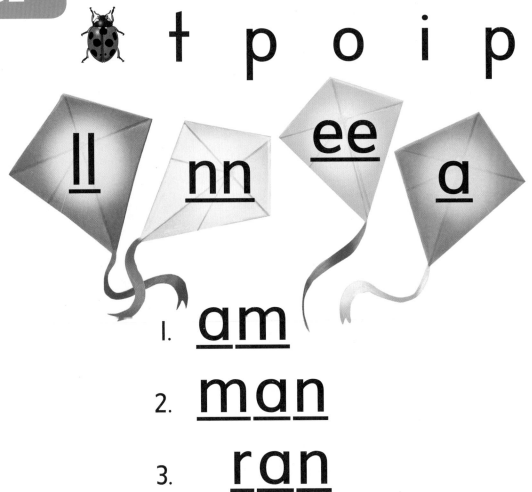

t p o i p

ll nn ee a

1. <u>am</u>
2. <u>man</u>
3. <u>ran</u>

<u>for</u>

<u>seem</u>

25

y i e t p y

1. <u>am</u>
2. <u>ran</u>
3. <u>me</u>

<u>oa</u> <u>ea</u>

26

1. <u>s</u>eem 2. <u>f</u>eel

1. <u>r</u><u>am</u>
2. <u>me</u>
3. <u>seen</u>

<u>ai</u>   <u>oa</u>   <u>ea</u>

1. <u>am</u>
2. <u>me</u>
3. <u>no</u>

29

p e y o a y

t f r s t n

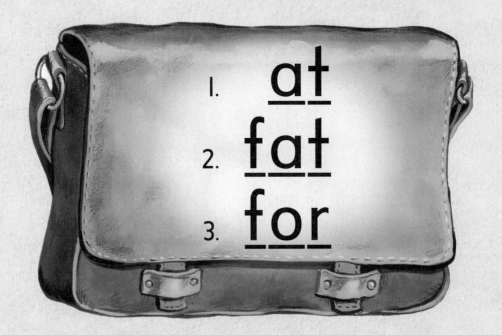

1. <u>at</u>

2. <u>fat</u>

3. <u>for</u>

<u>ea</u> <u>oa</u>

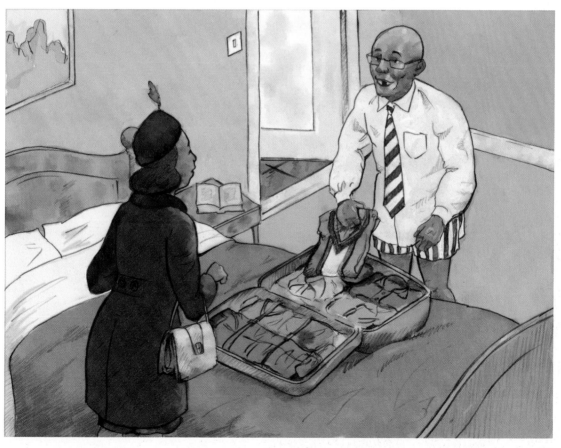

a p i y

l t f r t

1. <u>or</u>

2. <u>for</u>

3. <u>am</u>

4. <u>ram</u>

e
o
a

oa
ai
ea

h r t h

a f o t r ee

ai

ed

1. <u>man</u>

2. <u>mat</u>

3. <u>feel</u>

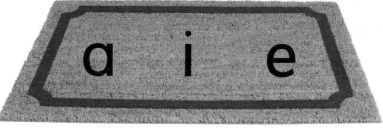

a i e

r y p h t n h f y

e_a_

_a_i

1. m**e**_a_n
2. r_a_in
3. m_a_il

1. see
2. no
3. man

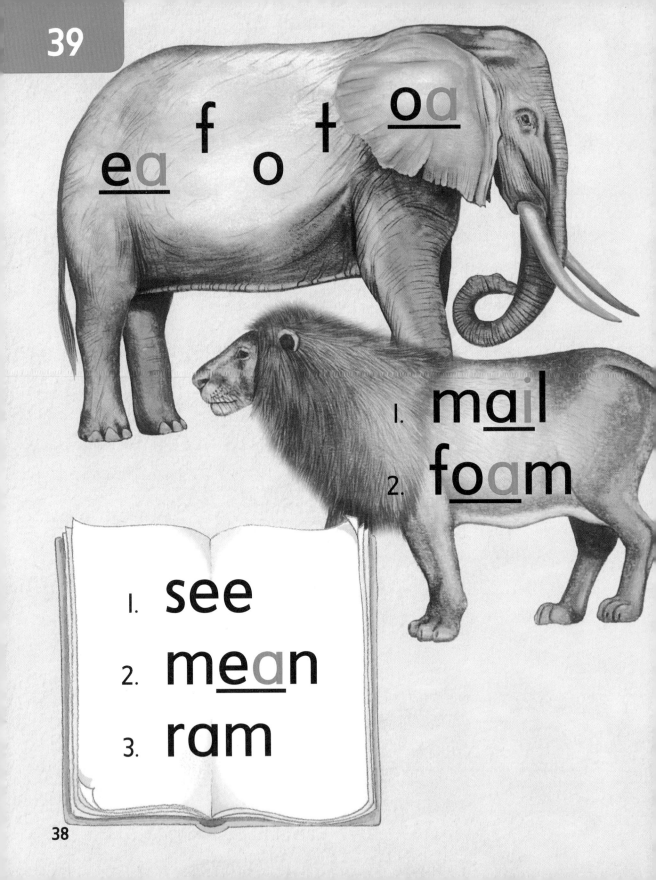

e̲a f o t o̲a̲

1. m a̲ i l
2. f o̲ a̲ m

1. see
2. m e̲ a̲ n
3. ram

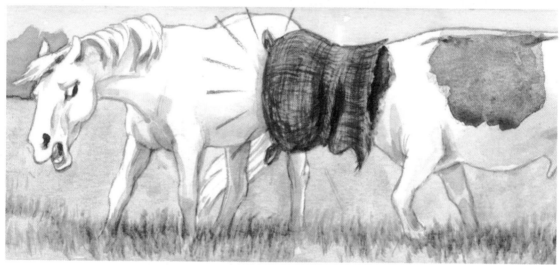

ai ea t oa

1. f**oa**m

2. s**ea**l

3. r**ea**l

1. ram

2. Sam

3. am

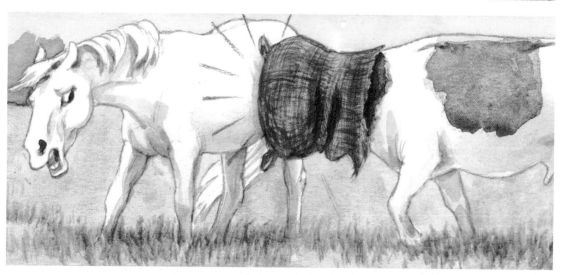

I a rmlin

1. lo**af**
2. se**al**
3. r**ai**n
4. m**ea**n

1. am
2. ram
3. m<u>e</u><u>a</u>n

43

I a

1. r**ai**n
2. m**ea**l
3. l**oa**f

1. I see
2. a m**ea**l

a I

1. f<u>o</u><u>a</u>m
2. r<u>e</u><u>a</u>l
3. t<u>ai</u>l

1. I am
2. a ram
3. I am m<u>e</u><u>a</u>n.

46

47

1. **my**
2. **fly**

1. <u>ea</u>t
2. n<u>ea</u>t
3. s<u>ai</u>l

1. I am Sam.
2. at me

y   f   e   y   o

1. try
2. my
3. fly

1. n<u>ai</u>l
2. s<u>ea</u>l
3. s<u>ai</u>l

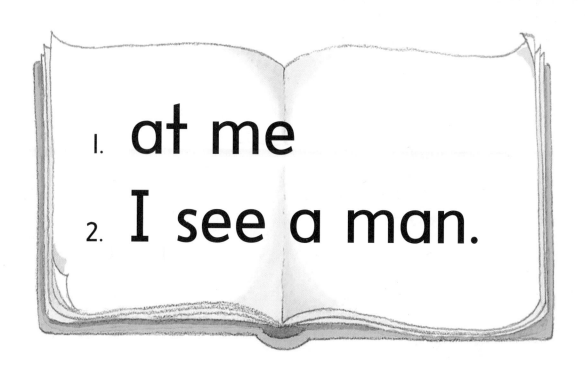

1. at me
2. I see a man.

I see a man.

47

1. A ram
2. A sail

1. fly
2. try
3. my

1. mail
2. loaf
3. eat

1. I eat.
2. I eat a loaf.

52

1. A t<u>ai</u>l
2. A fan

1. fry
2. try

1. s<u>ea</u>t
2. s<u>ai</u>l
3. s<u>ea</u>l

1. I <u>ea</u>t a l<u>oa</u>f.

2. I sat.

t s p f

1. feel
2. e**at**
3. n**ai**l
4. l**oa**n

1. **ea**r
2. n**ea**r
3. for

57

1. I see no man.

2. My fan ran.

1

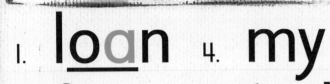

1. l<u>oa</u>n
2. for
3. ant

4. my
5. t<u>ai</u>l

1. <u>ea</u>r
2. t<u>ea</u>r

1. I see no ant.
2. I feel an ant.

p a y p i

1. **pal**
2. **l<u>ea</u>p**
3. **s<u>oa</u>p**

1. fine
2. mile

1. sail   2. seal   3. neat

1. See me s<u>ai</u>l.

2. I am a s<u>ea</u>l.

See me s<u>ai</u>l.

p ai y ea i oa

1. fry

2. spy

1. ate

2. fine

3. safe

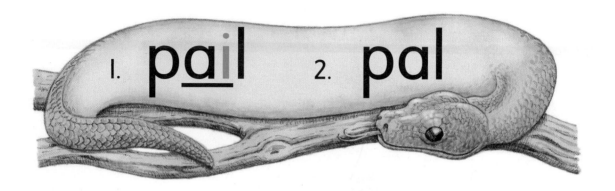

1. p<u>ai</u>l   2. pal

1. I feel r<u>ai</u>n.

2. See me s<u>ai</u>l.

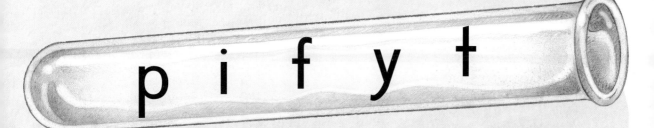

p i f y t

1. pal
2. pan
3. s<u>oa</u>p
4. fly

1. mile
2. note
3. late

See my pal eat.

oa y ea i ai

1. fly

2. fry

3. try

1. mole

2. ate

3. fine

1. ate 2. at

I am n**e**a**r** my pal.

a i p o d t e a y

1. at
2. sat
3. rat

1. pan
2. tan
3. n<u>e</u><u>a</u>r
4. m<u>a</u><u>i</u>l

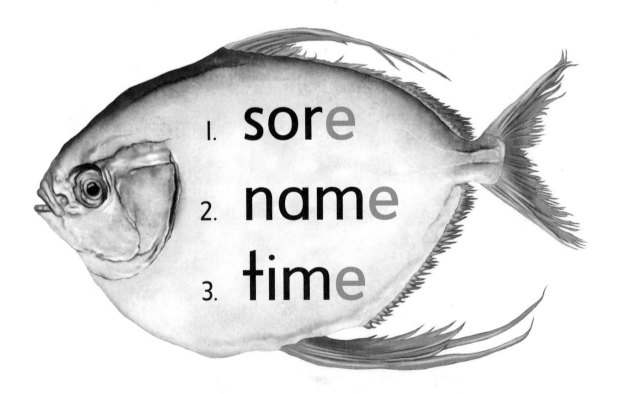

1. sore
2. name
3. time

1. A ram ran at me.
2. I ran at a ram.

1. A ram ran at me.
2. I ran at a ram.

th y p o a t th ai

1. <u>ea</u>r

2. an

3. or

4. feet

1. sat 2. safe
3. ate 4. at

1. I am safe.

2. My feet feel fine.

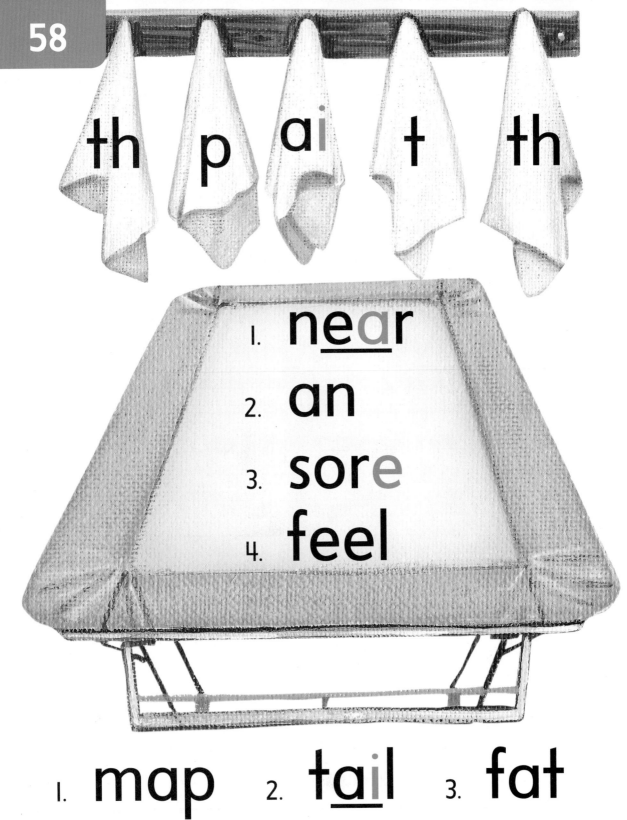

th p ai t th

1. n**ea**r
2. an
3. sor**e**
4. feel

1. map 2. t**ai**l 3. fat

1. I feel r<u>a</u>i<u>n</u>.

2. My feet feel fine.

y i th ai p t th

1. fly
2. ne**ar**
3. feet
4. sat

1. Sam
2. sam**e**
3. nam**e**
4. mor**e**

1. pal
2. p**ai**l
3. pil**e**

1. A fly sat n**e**_a_r me.

2. My feet feel sor**e**.